MILES PRESS

Indiana University South Bend Department of English

WE CAN'T TELL IF THE CONSTELLATIONS LOVE US

42 Miles Press
Editor, David Dodd Lee
Copyright© 2023 Jennifer Oakes. All rights reserved.
ISBN: 978-1-7328511-5-3 (pbk. alk. paper)

For permission, required to reprint or broadcast more than several lines, write to:
42 Miles Press, Department of English, Indiana University South Bend
1700 Mishawaka Avenue, South Bend, IN 46615

http://42miles.wordpress.com

Art Direction: Paul Sizer, Design: Jade Sibley, Production: Paul Sizer
The Design Center, Frostic School Of Art, Western Michigan University.
Printing: Sheridan Saline, Inc.

WE CAN'T TELL
IF THE
CONSTELLATIONS
LOVE US

POEMS
BY
JENNIFER
OAKES

CONTENTS

1.

2.

For my sisters—Patricia, Jess, Janice, Nance, and for Gavia

1.

THE FILM

The future rubs itself on the world and leaves
a film. You look outside.

Trees are where birds
separate themselves from the sky.

Everyone needs a break from the distances
we have placed between us.
Your mother calls you so you can explain the plot
of a book she doesn't understand
because the movie made no sense.
Other people are wiping their faces on the salesgirls
to prove that their breath carries freedom.

Each tree seems to accept the world as it is.

A person you could love is
feeling his lungs to see if there is enough air
left for promises.

THE COMPLICATION OF MULTIPLE LIVES

Five states away my father says the sun
is making chicken.
His cancer opens a shadow hand
in his brain. What the hand touches,
the world slides sideways.
He watches his window like a television
that plays reruns of the 1940s:
the tree, the road, the still air.
Back where I live, we're trying
to figure out how to order pizza
the way we used to before a teacher
explained sex to our daughter:
It's like pizza, she said, everyone likes it,
but with different toppings,
and you have to talk about what you want
before you order.

Now we just go hungry from laughing
too hard to make the call. So what

if language doesn't quite work any more,
or works so much that it means anything?
When I visit my father,
he tells me he misses the hair of branches
on the blazing bar.
I admit I too miss the leaves
and those trees we planted together,
and it's alright if he can't reply,
if the words just fall out.
He sleeps.
                    I return home. I am blue,
so I tell my daughter it's like a falling barn.
I mean life, but it sounds like
I'm talking about pizza, or sex.

Then I say Whoa, check out that flowering field,
and that sounds like it's about sex too,
which makes us laugh, which makes me cry.

We name every item in the entire world
and it's like we're giving birth to sex every time
we point to something.
    The bone is bleached by the sun.
    The hawk is circling its prey.
    It's always hottest in August.
All of the sentences mean and do not mean.
The whole time, my father is trying
to make one real sentence: he says death,
he says death, he says death
is different from winter. He's dying.

We drive past all the places we might go someday.

My father scratches at the window and dies.
We go on living. I love everything
disastrously. Whoever you are, the trees
have always been on fire.

WE CAN'T TELL IF THE CONSTELLATIONS LOVE US

There is smoke
covering the stars
so we can't tell
if the constellations love us
and will let us keep this home.

Dear Sky,
do you remember bison?
Whose back are you scratching now
that they are gone?

In the photograph
their skulls were climbed
like a ladder
to a broken phone.

Air lived inside all the eyes.
In a pile like that
it can be hard to see
that the world is connected
by breath
and it's bodies that do
the breathing.

WHAT WE DID INSTEAD

One personal reproductive theory
is that
            if my husband and I had installed a device
under our bed, programmed so a thrust-
activated movement sensor
would trigger a voice
that would cry out "war, war, war"—if we'd done
that—we wouldn't have
our daughter now.

My husband, who has one heart that shines
on the table of all possible hearts,
would have had to fold up his penis
and put it away until the sensor broke
or we forced ourselves to pretend
that the word *war* was just another word
for *shake your ass*, or *hold it there*, or *next time
let's eat chicken while we do this*.

I noticed in the paper
how the runway models were thin again
and blackeyed
            in clothing so shredded it wouldn't get stolen
in a refugee camp. I think it means something

that lately when I put on my shoes
I think: Do these work
for fleeing a homeland? Are they too easy
to steal from my exhausted feet?
Lately, my boots lace to the knees.

Airplanes were exploding our towers
so we could get on with war.
We hadn't installed a sensor machine,

but we heard war in every door opening, every bite
into fruit. We were slick with it.

    We did not install
    the machine. What we did instead
was go to Minnesota in the middle of winter
where it was so cold that the fish
we hauled up through the ice holes
were just green logs with eyes.

We cut them open
and threw their guts at winter
where the birds ate them. We were there
to visit my family, all just in from the frozen lake
of the blue-green fish,
and I was a few beers under with an egg
on its way.
For a moment as I stood with my husband
among my people
who were breading the fish
and humming and slapping their thighs
by the fire, there was no war anywhere.
I mean this is what we had
at that moment:

          food, fire, a game
on the wood table where people pressed
buzzers and flipped the timer, laughing. We turned away

to head upstairs to the room we shared.
We closed the door. We lay down
where no one had thought to install a machine,
and we made one child and had to watch
her open as the world entered bit by bit,
and the world was sharp where she was best.

STREET OF THE NEXT POSSIBLE WAR

Once each thing becomes a street,
you can walk anywhere. Yes
you can turn down Ash Place
or Manning Avenue but also yes
there are streets of fence posts and flour,
shock collars and hubcaps.
Find their roads, and you can enter.

Without looking where I was going,
I turned onto the street of autumn,
which hurt me because that is where
the farmhouse of my childhood lives.
Its kitchen sang in persimmon
cupboard drawers. A red barn.
A lake where cows swam
to meet our sinking boat.
There was a bell to call us in for food
and a velvet chair for company.

It was the place where the trees remembered
my breath, and it was sold.
My daughter asked once
if she will ever know war in her heart.

I was driving when she asked me that
and I thought of that house, sold
and cleared out during the month
I went away. I was told I could visit
if I ever found myself
near that place again. So the answer
was yes.   The war
in your heart will have a name,
the name of the street
by which you enter what you love.

There are birds in this world
that will blister your ears
or blind your soft parts.
Their songs and the songs of all the rest
will leave you if you shoot too many.

On my street I knew cardinals and geese,
wrens, the shining grackle. I jumped
from the barn's roof holding feathers.
I fell but nothing broke. It was so fast.
It is how we live atop this rushing earth.

LUNAR YEAR OF THE EXPLOSION

The people are shooting the sky
again tonight.

When it dies,
its body will be a hallway of our dreams:

a woman washing her head, a goat
looking down from the awning,

a purse spilling the fish we lost
when we told the rivers to double their haul

if they wanted to live. All the things
in our dreams have grown arms.

When they reach for us, it is
to hold us tenderly.

It was not always terrible
to be held to our making.

At their chests, we understand
why we took their teeth,

blunted their claws, dimmed their voices
into a shroud between the worlds.

FIRST PENIS

I slipped it soft
into the pages of a book, flaccid

marker of the page
where characters sifted trash for seeds and long
roots, sifted for string, for jar lids. For

years the penis remained shut
between the pages, bookmark to the vision
of an oncoming world.

But the things of this world are impossible
not to rub against,

and sometimes
at the mention of where trees and cows had lived,
and where hammocks grazed the air,

the penis would swell and force open
the pages, laying flat the book.   Then,

the breeze flipped pages one way
then back the other, telling the story forward
and back.

This was how the penis learned of time. It could
become a story told in reverse

where the girl holding the nail would first need
to look for it if she wanted ever to be born
among the rubble.

AFTER FIFTEEN YEARS, I WRITE ABOUT MY HOME

Will we still have fern
leaf beech. Will there be algae
in the next place,
fire, a forest of arms. See
how the plum falls when the wasp
enters. The least weight
and it falls. I will carry that
to the next house.
That, and the way the cougar
crossed a river
to avoid my daughter's
grief over leaving. Will
it always be leaving,
will it always be fear.
I stopped asking water, stopped
asking roots. And they let me
go. This is how to do it: ask nothing
and the world will let you
leave. It will tell you when
you have arrived.

LET ME SEE IF I HAVE THAT ADDRESS

Take it as a good sign
if no one mentions your entire species
on the news. Once that happens,
people press in for the scenery
of the vanishing world in ruins, watching
what it looks like as the remnants
drag themselves into extinction.

By the time we mention a war, its people are already
dead. We got the message. To name a thing
is to say goodbye.

Spotted owl, rhino, polar bear.
                    I hate to do this, but salmon,
tiger, island marble butterfly.
Animals with impossible necks, spots
like splotches of soup, movement
to the next branch slow as winter crank.

I once wrote grandmother.
I once said eternity. I wrote house, father, shining
floor. I said water. I said deer who accepts
the apple from my hand. I said human
voice on the other end of the phone.

I like the trees where fruit rots
so the birds can get drunk too.
What of this beautiful place
should we not pin to the map next so it will be
discovered? Olive grove, ice sheet,
carcass on the watered lawn.

EAR TAG

At the weigh-in, the guy with the puncher
kept trying to jam the tag
through the ear of the cow. Again.
The puncher was stuck or dull. The cow groaned
against her pen.   Again.
The kid who tried to calm her
ended up kicking his sister instead.
We all saw that moment, the cow
most of all: how she had been herself,
and then the tag went in, and then
she was made of numbers. Her eyes, the spool
of saliva unraveling across her face
when she tossed her head back again. Again.

She came to my dream
where dogs were tearing a couch apart.
We threw rocks to beat back the dogs.
We called 911. We wanted
to save her. To save just one thing.

In the dream I made my daughter
stay in the car. Maybe this is about marriage.
Maybe it's about icebergs
or the memory of my father. Maybe it's the cow.
Let's just say there is a big thing.

My daughter wore her seatbelt
the whole time with the windows up
and never once asked what we were doing.

WE ARE ALL WANDERING THROUGH THE GUTS

The city:
Sky held from the grasses. How they loved.

> When looking for a body, always turn to the unpaved parts
> : where it came from.

Should we make a building?
How much sky will it erase

in the anatomy of light and wiring
where there had been wings, had been sugar

full of bees.
Their song is under the city: old meadow, old meadow—

.   .   .
The meadow body under that city

is like parchment: each layer light-skimmed
and thick as the lake's skin which is lake all the way through.

Meadow edge, you hold a city.
Meadow edge, you are a box of light with streets squirming out

like the long, white
worms who understand when a body is final.

Remember the story of the mother goat who cut her children
from the body of the wolf and sewed stones into his belly

to fool him. He woke up thirsty
and fell into the well.

He was so heavy. The stones called themselves back
to the place of their first eruption.

I first read this story in a library. How I loved again
the scissors and the thread.

SALT COUSINS

I moved to the island because
on the mainland the street lights

made clown faces bloom in the puddles
and the cats rubbed themselves
on my garden.

Once I was surrounded by ocean I was happy
to be at last alone among water who was my first home.
Cells, I said, go play with your salt cousins.

Stars came out and did their thing on the ocean.
The whales swallowed patches of things
in the water and lived or died.

Everything found an approximate match to itself
in the dark.

Eventually we all became more of what we already were:
I made more me, plastic made more plastic,
leaves rubbed together
and other leaves came out.

At some point I noted the stars barely take up any space
if you make your eyes into slits.

The ocean said its whales sometimes swallow constellations.
It gave me a few bottles to pick up from the shore
so I could throw them at the sky
to make more sky.

All the cell cousins said we weren't safe
once that started. We're salt, too, I said, we're family.

2.

THE END OF MEMORY

He explains again how he lived in a city
where they sold turtles on Thursdays,
though we suspect this was a story
read to him years ago by a sister whose name
now empties his mouth like a puff.
He sometimes remembers a scar
from a hay hook but not which cousin
wears it. And when the neighbor calls,
he recognizes her freckles but not her face.

What we have is only what we are given
at that moment: later, when the forgetting begins,
the details that remain surprise us—
a button, a borrowed shovel. It's all new
and we turn it over like a bucket.

We eat and forget and eat again.
The dog loves it. The dog runs around
and tells us everyone is hungry again:
time to eat. It's a beautiful feast
when the beast with the longest fur
is in charge.
                    We tie our bibs
and reach for the warm piles on the plates.
We ask the walls for advice
because they see what we see
with the same blankness.
Nothing we say to them
makes them rearrange their faces.
We love them for that.

When we can't remember caress
we say carcass. When we can't recall
Field and Stream we say Fraud and Stain.
Have we read it?
We keep reading it, many times.
Someone must keep handing it
to us. Its pages rustle like a dry well,
by which we mean a dry field,
a field where lightning could ignite the world

if you could remember how to get there
and be lightning.

SO SHINY IT IS HARD TO BELIEVE

Here's to the year of the baby seal,
coinciding with the Year of Saving the Liver, which follows
the years of the exploding glass

doors and cars that wouldn't stay
on straight. Sorry, bottles.   Sorry, emptiness
sloshing around in there. Amazing

how fast what empties from one place
fills another: see the bin of empties,

bottle red of my face, see the cellular slag
of how every moment can become a reason to fill another cup.

                              Is it time to apologize
for how present the everywhere is?

The vastness which is throatlike
in its swallow?   Breakage
is just another form of becoming.

At the ocean there is glass on every beach.
And then there's how sand is made from bottles
like the whole world was poured out
on the rocks.

I am going around with a bag
to gather the seaglass because
it recognizes me.

I have to cradle my liver like a seal.

It asks me nothing.   It has dark eyes.

They are so shiny it is hard

to believe we used to look past them
to club the mother first.
The pup didn't know to be afraid,
so stayed and made the young sounds of water.

IN MY ORIGINAL KANSAS, WHEN WE WERE IRON

First there was how my brain
was blanked by the depression.
Drinking to bring the brain back
makes you wake up
forgetting how to read. I forgot
the word for face, forgot
how to turn napkins
into animals and if
the stars still made silver.

Thank you for asking,
but before I could write
to tell you how I'm doing,
I had to learn to drive past
neon lights and liquor stores
and to stand upright at parties
without putting my hands
down people's pants or asking
if the corner near the clustered plants
was a good place for crying.

I came back and remembered
words that lived in my original Kansas.

The Kansas we knew 500 years ago
when we were a wagon wheel
and a stick-dragged line—
and the Kansas of all the years before that,
from the Big Bang through to protozoa

and right up to the moment
of having arms and air freshener
so when we sell our houses
it smells like we learned to cook.

I came back and am learning
to make pizza from a box.
I am ordering boxes
and am grateful for how much they do.
They produce food and clothing
and build towers in the garage.
They are how we get so many things
into our houses: boxes arrive on the porch
and inside of them is a whole life
you can just switch on with a remote
or hang from walls or eat. Hams
and snack cakes. Harmonicas.
Buckets for throwing up.
I am learning kale. I am learning soup
and how to make it
without using a can
opener as the stirring spoon.
I am learning that an empty box
is the daughter's magic castle
whose wish is that you will remember
how not to sleep.

After the long depression
I had three selves:

the one who can still feel
the ungraspable edges and the sliding down,
the one who believed it was over
and so threw flowers at the sun,
and the one who saw those first two
selves from the great distance
and felt the tenderness
of inevitability: I would happen
to myself again
and I would happen to myself
again, and this meant
goodbye, goodbye, goodbye.

This meant ants on the meat tray.
This meant friends
who write to ask where I am.
How should I know?

I am in three places.
We are all crossing the street together:
the first self afraid to be hit by the car,
the second just happy
to know the word for street
because it is enough some days
to have a single word.
And the third who understands
both that the car will hurt
and that the street is a long way away
because I am also a sky. I am a sky

the same way I am Kansas: a body
of dust, a body of evaporate and dissipate
and windblown brick.
Kansas in my dog blood.
Kansas before it was named.

I arrived there because it was already in me.
Little Kansas, it said, and I arrived
into myself and into the good red dirt,
the good brown dirt, the dirt of departures
blown in from the far side
of the country, passing through, settling,
and moving on.

Little Kansas, you are dragging a stick
to find your way back,
but the wind says no.
The trail you scraped
showing the way back is blown over
so now your arrival is everywhere.
The dirt of my self / Dirt of where to plant next.

Thank you for asking how I am doing.
It hadn't occurred to me
that the question could feel so active:
the *doing* part.
I am putting books in boxes.
I am packing up my daughter's room.
I am asking the spoons not to multiply.

I am separating light from dark
as if morning is not a season.
Doctors agree that mornings
are the most difficult.
That's when the lying begins
about how the day will go, a day
when I remain fully dressed and upright
among pine trees or people with nothing
but gorgeous coffee in that cup.
This is all before a bird hits the window
and the whole plan unravels
and then you have to apologize
to the plates for throwing them.
They shouldn't have to break like that.
No one should break like that.

Sometimes I am grateful for my vanity.
I used to hate it: the way I ran
from one shadow to the next
so the sun wouldn't fill my skin
with Kansas. But then I read
how drinking and weeping sags
the jowls and bursts the veins
and that was another reason
to quit. Now I smile
even while reading the terrible news
because I need to make smile lines.
If there is still beauty available,
I want to give it a chance, make

a path for it to come in on.
Dear Beauty: you have a week
to arrive. After that, all promises
are radio static, they're snow in May.

After that, I may fall in love again
with my sheets. They are the hotel
of my dreams.
There, my drowning self can miss
entire life cycles of frogs.
My singing self would like to see them hatch.
And the faraway self understands
the frogs will emerge again
and then again, each year
until one of those other selves
has won. The winning self will declare
which one I finally am:
The Sleeper, The Singer?
I may become the one who rises
for polliwogs and hears
flagellate pulsings encoded by star-speak.
No, I may sleep in tadpole darkness
and miss their forthcoming selves. Perhaps
I will be the one who makes small hats
for each of them and calls them
by their first name: Home.

I have been to Kansas my whole evolutionary history.
I have been a sky and a bed,
and they are not that different.

In Kansas, the earth is blown into bricks
and stacked until summer is an oven.

It is where animals come in trucks.
It is permitted to boil animals in Kansas, to clarify
their blood and sell it in bricks
for soup and for the heart,
which desires to be coursed through
by blood.

I also should ask how you are doing
except I can't recall
what we shared between us.
It was a wet sheet in August,
a haircut in September.
I entered Kansas
before there was lice on earth,
and stayed until the lice were complete,
eventually picked out by hands
that dot-to-dotted me
back together, calling me daughter daughter,
sister sister, mother mother.
When they talk to you like that,
it is hard to say no
to waking up. In this world.

In this world. Where the food
can't grow itself.
Where your elders are asking
where they're from. Where the concrete

is as close as the city kids will ever get
to a mountain: Mount Incremental Loss.
Mount Wagonload of Mountain
Until the Mountain is Gone.

You can be many things
if you listen to where your blood
has lived before it became so personal:
so person bound. Before that,
had you been the rain much?
Had you answered ink
with a wobbling song?
Does iron remind you of any other bloods you know?
Do you remember how to let go
of your feathers?
It's a muscle release, the letting go,
so the body can escape
into the underbrush.
Your rising sap self,
your microscopic cellular self.

You were so small before blood
found a way into you,
but you were always on the way.

I remember we shared some iron.

It was when our meteor selves
traveled to get here. We had to slam
into earth to make this life happen,
the constellations at our backs.

The world made shapes
out of oncoming you
and reshaped them right up until you,
and will go on shaping them after. Remember

when we arrived in Kansas
on our own hooves,
meat heavy and reading the grass
that was printed on the air.
Water was a cluster place
and we found it with our flat-toothed mouths,
our muzzle-soft faces. We looked at the stars
and divided. I was nickel. I was heave.
I was iron red and an ocean full of shapes
who still remember us.

We looked at the stars
and made more of them
from our ungulate lowing.
We were on the way to now.
The glaciers dropped their stones
and called it sleep. Thanks for asking

how I am doing. I am not sure
that today will be the kind of day
where the road works.
I'm not sure it's straight enough
to get us to the next city
full of my boxes. When I lived
in Kansas, it was redundant: just what happened
because I couldn't remember

my blood had been there already.
It called me back and I went
because I couldn't remember
I'd been there since the beginning.

When you don't remember
your original Kansas nothing goes
right. Charles drank everything
and almost died and Steven ate steak
on Valentine's Day because meat
was the only thing that sent him notes
written in red, and Karl just kept
getting married.
Were we the slowest cluster ever?
Stars that divided and divided
or got sucked back into themselves
and went cold?

Time led up to now, to this
world where the cows arrived in Kansas
by truck so we could eat them faster
and not have to see their star eyes,
their I-was-you-once faces.
In Kansas, they process the animals
and it smelled like scorched coffee
until I saw the processing floor and then
it smelled like memory loss.

Once on the cutting floor
I saw a long red braid

in the corner mixed with blood.
I wanted to know—I still want to know—
if whoever had worn that braid
cut it to get away from that room
or just ran out of things to cut. And so cut.

Who leaves such a history
to the scouring hose?
How long could I last on top of this blowing earth.

Thank you for asking. Sometimes
I am nowhere and sometimes
I become a place.

What of trucking in the animals
to cluster them to our hunger?
They ask for water at the slaughter house,
and no one answers them with water.
Before all that Kansas growing in us,
we could have been water.
Our hunger could have been their cluster place.
We could have gone to them. It is easy
to be water. It's like downhill.
It's like sugar.

You looked
like stars as you divided and divided.
They call you brother brother.
If you can't hear them, ask your blood
who will answer them with iron.

I appreciate that you asked, because
it means I am still here.
I could not always say that.
Not when I was gone, just before
I became the three selves. You will wonder
what opened up to let those selves through.

That's what I'm telling you.
It's the first Kansas. It drew me
to it and let me go. Come back,
it said, and I came back.
Go now, it said, and I left
but could not find my way.
Draw your cells as circles, it said,
and I did.
Follow their magnetic pull, it said,
and I went west until I had a baby
who drew circles and crossed them all
out, and my friend feared
that they were eyes and tried
to wake me up. He must have known me
when we were sand.

When I asked him if we'd hit Kansas yet,
he said we'd never left. It is all the same.

When they handed us water we bloomed
and I feared the bloom.
I went into water and understood

I was water already. I drank it
because I know how to drink
whatever is near or in my hand.
I drank the water and water
and water until I
always had water in my hand
and nothing else, until I became
the cluster place of my own gathering
and the cluster place of star blood.

And when my daughter asked
if I was now able to walk
with her to the top of a hill
for the first day of spring, I said
yes. I said yes, yes, I said yes
because I knew how
to get there, and because I knew
the long way down.

WHERE WE REACH, A FACE WILL RISE TO MEET THE HAND

Even after my friend got stung
by a wasp and fell from the tree,
and the whole thing went bad
and he lost his arm

everyone says don't worry: we should
let our children go on climbing trees.
Perhaps they are right—
I should give trees to my daughter's childhood.

But who can stand
to lose more than they can pay for?

There was that decade when I couldn't spell
my own heart because it had no shape
in my mouth, it was empty there,
like the way the neighbor sometimes
touches her eyes
when she feels finished from so much
seeing. I came back
from that time. I stay petlike with safety
and am no longer made of fire.

Friend, when you were stung
and then fell from the tree,
what was the last note your hand wrote
as it traveled through that sky's uncomplicated blue?
Friend, I love arms.
How just one cell
eventually makes two of them.
How they can make flying
just by opening.

I DREAM YOU TO BE WELL

We are down to pan scrapings.
Leaves for stuffing and warmth.

Waxed paper holds heat differently
than paper without.
Tallow holds too, but also differently,

and attracts animals who
understand how we are all trained
to look for heat in calories or each other.
It is possible—   It is,

to buy one chicken and eat it
for the rest of your life,

to write with a feather
the name of your bird-self,
your scratch-self, your yolk-
self of future flight.

Thank you for dreaming me
to be well. I have a girl half my size
who lives off what I enable
to reach her.
                It is a world
where in the morning the birds
are gigantic and fall from trees
for the seeds in our hands
when there is seed.
And then for our hands
when our hands are empty.

WE CAN CLIMB THE TREES AND CALL OUT
HOW FAR WE SEE

People will look into your mouth
when you eat to see how much
like them you are: Do you
have teeth. Do you have breath.
Is there still a tongue
that makes pink shapes.
My father died and I keep
remembering things to tell him:
How we're planting trees
even though we all know
what birds sound like when
they hit the ground.
How we're tying hope to my daughter
by making chicken houses
even though the sun is always hotter.
Apples in the orchard. The wasp
makes a home in a plum. What I need
from everyone I love is to measure up
to your knees so you know where
the ocean will be one day,
and then I need you to just be taller than knees.
It's a simple ask. Mostly what I need
of anyone is that they be alive.

3.

WHAT THE BULLET TEACHES US OF LOVE

And perhaps the bullet is how we learn
we got the backward universe, not the one
that's expanding, but the one that contracts
and pulls back in over us.   Dear Gatling, you invented
a gun that shoots thirty-three hundred times
per minute. Thank you
for proving futility. Your invention reorders time
to your new scale: fifty-five bullets per second
means the second is no longer
a count of one, one, one, but now becomes
a moment that opens fifty-five times.
Gatling, we want our old second back,
the small dots of time that led to *minute*,
led to a pause over
bread.   Hold me.
How we fall when time becomes so split, so opened.

And perhaps this is what the bullet
teaches us of love: in bullet time, love happens in reverse
(*reverse in happens love / love of us teaches bullet*).

The last time I found love
in forward time,

                    I closed my eyes to feel
the static of the not-yet touching
of our mouths where a single second opened.
The second was long enough to allow desire
be the tuning, to let that first touch be the tuning.

And when that second passed the next one opened:
summer and hot, the lip-clung lip
and the June bug's heavy landing
into the flashlit halo. One more second,

and a muffler revved night's heavy engine
across the tongue's syrup search
for morning, spine-
bridge crossing one body to the other.

One day our world will say, Remember when
the plane with the Gatling gun flew by
and took our last minute made of seconds?
Remember seconds? We were alive then.
Gatling meant for his gun to shoot
so fast it would make war
obsolete.

:

What does time become when it passes
through a bullet hole to get here?
My gorgeous minute now
has thirty-three hundred ways to gape.
My round second, a frame for fifty-five holes.
How many times can we shoot the sky?

Dear love: that night we met was a glass
of whiskey, a gravel path, and some mint.

The curve of your foot
on my foot made me look for a closet,
a corner, an anywhere to hide our bodies and continue.
If you were a flare, I was oxygen in the canopy.
I wanted the trail we walked on
embedded in my back, the stars
to understand their light was not wasted
where it touched us. That touch was one second long.

Love, hold up any single second of our first minute,
and it was already a full life extending
all the way to Here. Dear you, we lived.
Dear you, I love your baby. I love her forward
in the old way. It is a gift.

I am grateful I got to love before I learned
of Gatling time, before time could be measured
in Gatlings. I got to love
before time became a string of rounds
that needed a shovel
to get rid of pileup. In Gatling time

each moment is thin-sliced so sheer
it will be called a Gatling cloth.
Dr. Gatling, you could not shoot fast enough
to prove the futility of war as you'd hoped.
Now Gatling is a round we crank. Gatling
the unit of shells, the shovel's worth of heave.

Count to one, and fifty-five rounds fall out.
           Oh minute, oh second, oh once-
bodies whole and solid.

In time that fast, it is no longer one mouth
on another mouth, but one nerve ending,
one fiber, one synaptic spark beyond
the myelin sheath into—
nothing yet: that would be the next
one thirty-three hundredth of a second. Leap
with me here. There are desires
that can be sliced that thin.
There are countries that will be so parsed.

Dear Gatling: How we love what disappears.

:

Dear Gatling,
You understood a world of love as better
and believed faster bullets would hurry peace.
I give you that. And true, when
the bullet teaches death, it also teaches
love. The Gospel According to Bullet
teaches the backwards order of things:
death then love, and I understand this finally
because loving in reverse
was how I was allowed to love Danny G,
son of people I never met because they left
for the weekend when their hot tub steamed
an open invitation into the minus-zero winter.

Danny put a towel in the dryer for me,
and we undressed. It was high school,
so nakedness was our best clothing.
We wore snow. Gatling, we wore sky-
black and lowlit stars: they were brilliant
but so far from us they lit us
where we glowed already.
Gatling, we wore water and steamed
when we stood, we were smoke bodies,
vaporous and rising.   When we wrote
the calligraphy of our bodies on the snow,
the snow-sting contracted our expanse
and returned us to our singular selves
until we re-entered the hot water
and bloomed again. Danny with his black curls.
Snowflake drift. Skin pale as rationing.
We closed our eyes. We

did. One minute. We were seventeen.
What we wore hovered over. Fog bodies,
steam driven selves, conductors
of the risen lakes.

Each flash of memory from that time
still happens in the old unit, the second.
I cannot remember faster, remember less.
We had mouths that did not yet work
for speaking. When we opened
them, we smelled metal and sunflowers.
Gatling, I closed my eyes. It was easy
as having skin. I closed my eyes.

It was easy as asking to let something live.
Take any second close to you: I released
a frog, I danced on a wooden box,
I told my sister we could share the memory,
I pulled a pin from my foot.

This is not about loving Danny—
that wouldn't happen until he died.
When I was seventeen, kissing was just
a form of introduction. Hello, my name
is breakfast which is why we're breathing
like this. My name is eyeliner and I love
how the inside of your car
makes me think of nothing.

Was Danny any different from the others?
We wanted singing skin.
He put a towel in the dryer.
He led me back from the stinging snow.
But was he different?
There was James who made maps
of the places where he thought of me.
And Reggie who did not push the hook
through the worm, but loosened the earth
and returned it, and Jon who wrote my name
on his cymbals so he could play the sound of me
all night long. Danny died and they went on
living. This is how I learned of loving

in reverse: Danny gone is Danny dear,
Danny who comes to this poem
so words can still fall from his mouth.
The others have words of their own
and no other body they need.
Love this world, said Gatling: Shoot it faster
and so live.

Gatling, you're reading this
because in backwards time we learn to love
what's gone. Shoot something in the heart,
and everyone will love it more. In backwards time,
this letter practically unwrites itself.
I'll see you there, Gatling. Ask me to arrive
so I can walk backwards from you.
I am becoming too young
for paper. My mouth is hungry
for words. The people I miss are coming
to feed it. You still have time to uninvent yourself.

:

On the radio they headline the Gatling gun.
It's news, mounted to a fighter jet.
It has a hidden door that tells fifty-five secrets
per second.   One minute of secrets
writes a book.
                    Flip to any page   and die.

When the fighter jet's door flips up
it means the pilot is ready to engage.
How many holes   can a minute take
and just keep walking?

Danny crashed a plane into his twenties.
His last taffy seconds, a rubbery stretch
of time in whole notes and a slingshot stretch
of elastane dive. The earth so
                                        inarguable
as the lights of his plane made an amphitheater,
a tunnel of light where the final bloom was death.

There was a snowflake. I reached out my hand
and held it there. It took one second.
The towel made a single rotation in the dryer.
Three steps in the snow.
Maybe these each happened
in the same second: the snowflake, the towel,
the footsteps. I went home that night
and slept well because I had been in water
and kissed a boy I hoped might never call
because it had already been better
than having hands. We were in a hurry,
running first through winter
and then into lives where if we looked back,

we'd see that just before we kissed
the sky had already entered our mouths.

The lightyears crossed by the stars told us
how long it had taken just to be touched
by a human face, and we heard them.
Before I learned to kiss, every word
had been given to me by someone else.
But kissing occurred to me, the first form
of my first original, accurate word.
It was answered by exactly what it asked for.

I did not love Danny until his mouth was cold
and would always be crammed full of cold,
a closet where his mother hung
her crying, where his father stored the tuxedo
of his prayers. The everness of that space.
How bound we are to this earth,
and how much we need the dead
so we can learn to love. And now
we have them more than ever.
Have we fathomed? Have we
reckoned much? Have we learned
a fucking thing? The airplane's hidden door
holds this secret: the details will be erased
by holes. I am making popcorn,
I am rinsing my daughter's hair, I am asking
my father if he can hear the grackle.
How many times can we shoot those moments?

Time is a landscape of events. Slice one
to the three-thousandths of thin,

and you're holding a gossamer sheet,
one whose translucency makes it difficult
to identify the bodies, the winter, the night
which may or may not be the last thing
pressing down and down upon our faces.

Take that thin-sliced moment and hold it
up to the light so you can see it.

You have one second to scan for the details,
to remember them. Then fifty-five holes
begin their work.
                    What remains
once Gatling time begins? A dark curl, a three-
fingered hand. Keep looking—one next second—

and the Gatling cloth becomes a net.
It hauls time and disappears.

At ten seconds the moment's new story
is told by five hundred and fifty rounds
and we're not even halfway across the minute.
The body rendered ash-same as snow, ash-same
as towel, hair, or hand. Smoke bodies, vaporous
and sifting. Black curl of everywhere.

And then, on the other side of that second
you're holding up, you see
the other world. The faces

look at you from there, hands pressed over
the mouths of children. Not one   sound.
Not one breath.
                         The slightest movement
might trigger another second's worth
of time and split it

into rounds. Let time hold still long enough
to build a wall around that world, a roof,

long enough to pack some bread, gather shoes,
and flee. Stay still,
dear world of scattershot invention,
we can save you once we've healed the second.

But perhaps this is our job, to be
passed through. To be always
the thinnest slice of now.
My sister wiping corn from a table.
The neighbor setting keys in a bowl.
My parents counting the evening pills.
The latest Gatling gun is still in its test phase.

For now, it's being tested on the air
of this coming year. The sky is an occasion
to fill with holes. When that sky dies,
there will be another sky on the other side.

Danny is still falling. All the pilots are falling.
Their mouths are shaped like goodbye,
which tastes like history. There are ashes
in the radio. Each snowflake is a hotel
I want to sleep in. Can you still hear me
through the thickness of the second?
I'm still using old time, the dear second,
without permission

while the new guns measure
Gatlings. The engineers measure muzzle flash,
flying qualities, and human factors
to determine if they've achieved success.
When new seconds appear, they release
the rounds upon the minute. They record results
and try again.

When new time appears it is a target:

it can be shot so full you'd think
it had an identical twin of Never-was.
Time and his brother Other Time.
Shoot them both, and they reveal a triplet,
keep going and the world is a progeny of air.

This is how we love in reverse: this
is how we love the dead. Backwards.
Never so much. / *Much so never.*
The people who are falling from windows.

The boat of the sinking country. The gun
tells us we need to love faster. I love Sierra
Leone. I love Orlando and Paris, Sandy
Hook, I love you. In Gatling time we can't love
enough in the present moment.
In Gatling time, love is aftermath.

The old round is a place we carry
and hope to never spill.
Round of my daughter's head.
Round of fruit, of bowl, of hanging nest.
Round of lake's belly, of song
and plate and shining marble shoulder.
This is before research and development.
The new round is what gives
birth to bullet.

I need time in seconds because
there are so few of them I remember.
They need to weigh more, to be substantial
enough to hold. My sister in the doorway.
She remembers her orange pajamas
and her hair in curlers because on Christmas
we needed to wreathe the air with ringlets.
But then my father's brother
died before we opened presents.
The call came in. My sister in her curls
and orange pajamas. I remember
that the pajamas were actually mine

and I was the one who wore them.
Where I stood when the phone rang
is where my sister says she was:
the white doorway where the chips
in the paint made sailboat-shapes.
I could stand there long enough and sail away.
The wind, the asking to go into water.
I believe it is my memory
because I have never seen it in a photograph.

No one points the camera
at children when their uncle dies. His family heard
a sound and perhaps thought he was carrying
a giant present down the stairs.
They closed their eyes to wait for it, opened them—

and surprise, forty years and counting,
we're all waiting for a better gift.

For all of us, the heart became measured by time.
The entire loop of arteries and veins:
gush one way, pull the other. Time held
loop de loop. Until the springing open
from the heart: the opened round of time,
and then the world's phone rings and the children
in the doorway don't know if they should ask
if it is okay to still want to open presents
even though the adults are sagging
over their bones and the sailboats have left
for nowhere good.

Crying is round in the throat.
Uncle Chuck died and became a round place
in the chest. A dull ornament of winter.
Each room had a phone, all of them ringing
into the morning to convey the heart's new ruin.
We agreed to share the memory:
orange pajamas for everyone.
I need that minute of the ringing phone.
It found the heaviness of my mother's hands
and I remember them. I need that minute
because it is one of the few I have
where a memory still lives.

                          Were we supposed
to write childhood down? I woke up and forgot
the color of my bedroom. I held a spoon
at a table of uncertain shape. My dog
was named something brown. Did I love
bacon sizzle? Did I know oatmeal in the pot?
The sound of scissors as my hair fell
to the kitchen floor? I have not saved enough
of memory for what I need to survive
if I have to lift the details to the light,
thin-sliced. Thin already, they would not
make it through a single Gatling moment:
fifty-five holes and the little I have would disappear.

Purr of a cat, I remember you. Breakage
in the sink, I remember. Wine glass,
my father crying, I remember and no one held

a camera there. Ice skates under my pillow,
I recall. The sprint up from the barn
because the calf breathed like a factory
of wet blankets before it died.

I remember you, breathing. I remember you, calf.
Sound of skates on the lake, I hear you still.
Bread in the orange kitchen.
Velour in a bag. Jacket sleeping in the corner.

Childhood is loose rubble in old pockets.
Memory flash of a few frozen seconds.
Fifty-five holes, and there goes the doorway,
the orange pajamas, the tree-lit sister,
and those curls. And what else remains
after that first second? Fifty-five holes
and only the phone, ringing on our end,
the other connected to the home
where all together they can't lift the body
from the stairs. The body. When it was alive,
that was the gift they heard. They remember.

Will we help them? The sky remains.

Dear Gatling, leave me with the body,
the phone, my sister's spiral-perfect hair.
We will eat a silent dinner,
we will sleep amidst wrapped gifts
and wonder if inside of each of them

there is another phone with a thin-wired voice
confirming that our father is now the oldest
and will always be the oldest. Each
of his brothers and children have become
the oldest and will always be the oldest.
Leave me with my minute.
I need the details full and bodied.

Does the new time mean we are running
out of time? That when time becomes this thin
all that's left is a waiting sky?

Remove enough of what separates you
from the nearest sky, and the sky behind
will come to you. You can call it
Next Sky. It came from the round place
of its father and asks for him by name:
Gatling Round.

Dear Next Sky:
Your father died
the moment he reached for you.
A round is only a round until it is shot.
And this is how roundness
gives birth to a bullet. And this is how bullet
makes its hole: it must pass through round
and keep going until it is spent.
This is how a hole becomes death:
without asking.

Dear Next Sky:
In the old time, roundness lived
in the eyes of all our gods. They watched
from the sky until we shot through to the place
behind them. Now we see what they saw:
we look at time through a bullet hole
and the round is finished. I love your mouth.
I see how much you hold there
by the way the next word trembles
and waits for breath. I love how crumbs
are keys for the sparrows,
how dissection gathers us in circles.

We form communities around the bodies:
dear frog, you gathered us. Fetal pig,
and sheep's gray heart. These gatherings
happened in the last moments of the old round.
How they held us there. At the funeral
Uncle Chuck's body was still
the handsome one and gathered us
but the shape of us couldn't hold
because we kept breaking
from our centers. A round becomes
a space by hollowing.

:

Think of your life: each trajectory
so obvious once you play it in reverse.
Remember how your first air-mouth gathered

around its wail: round silence broken
by hunger for air. How the world's first milk
was air and let down to feed your lungs. You breathed.
Round in the lungs, round in the ears of crying.
Was it round in the arms? Your first breath out
lifted into the air of our own long-breathed world
and became the world's next breath.
New in its lungs.

Where do you feel the thinning? I mean
the places where we need repair:
Your mother asks how long she's known you,
if she's ever had divorce or children.
Her life is a curiosity now that it's a sky.
Was there religion? Was there swimming?
There's a song she's singing: she finds it odd
you know the words—only her children
would know that song, but she will share it
with you anyway. The song is so large inside her
that there's enough to go around. It's as though
she can fill forgetfulness with singing. Until
the voice goes thin in patches and comes out
struggling. Was there singing? Can you hear it

too? It used to gather people the way
pianos do, the way cows on a median strip,
the way gold, the way harvest, the way oil
and mass strandings and the only chair
in the room. Come to me: singing. Single note
hidden behind the parchment rasp,

what you gather now is sky: time is the bullet
through the once-round of voice. Child,
the song you meant to hold up to the light
had fifty-five notes in the first fourteen seconds.
It will not last: it will not last: it will not

    ,   ,

     .

Perhaps Gatling time will not find you
if you do not put what you love
near the shootable sky. Perhaps
if you ask better, or in a different voice.
A different language. Maybe if you say
the right thing and are wearing the jacket
everyone agrees on. Or maybe if you keep
the most important thing hidden. Fold it
and let your pocket swallow. Don't touch it there
or they'll ask to see it. Danny in the pocket dark.
The curl, the steaming winter, the towel
once around. Keep it safe, or it may become
the next hole through time, and disappear.

Is there muscle memory of sky?
You can feel it where you have been thinned.
My sister is a memory I want to keep.
My daughter is a round tension that arrows
my days. The tree where I learned to read
remains a round place even after
the people cut it down for a better view
of the lake. And this thins me.

Dear coming sky, I feel you there.
I feel you in my cut-tree sky self.
My blue car smashed self. Frozen dog
self. Dear Next Sky, you are already a tapestry
of scars. The lace of you. The blue behind blue
and all that weaving. Two years ago I held
myself together with bedsheets.
Wine bottles and the hope the green world
would ring me. That the blue sky would hold me
together because I could not.

It bound me with blue strips,
one blue behind the other, and always more
blue waiting. The torn jackets of skies
poured through the tearings to find me
until I was sky-pressed and contained.
Dear Sky, you are wrapped around me, and so
when I stand, you stand. You will be shot again,
and I will stitch you to the sky behind you
and rise, and you will go on standing.

Azure-jacket self, dropped-jar self,
back turned on the wounded-bear self:
dear Sky, we feel you
where we are no longer closed.
Our moments have been shot through
and we are seared to you. Dear Gatling:
we open where we hold the rounds of ourselves.
This is what you aimed for in your new time.
This is where we lived.

Gatling, have you yet heard
from the other side—those shot rather than
those who shoot? Those who live
on the other side have returned
to where all the original round is grown.
The old round, which lives in the faces
of leaves. In the places where our arms fold.
The place from where my father's voice lifts
when he says the names of fish.
It lives in butter's heart. In breath-catch
and apple bowl and the ringing tongues of steel.
Gatling, you live there now too. What
has the voice of iron said?

    That you have not released its round.
    That you have only rewritten time.

In our new time, we are orphans of round.
We will tell each new sky that we remember
the remnants of what it meant to be round.
The worm's path is a song.
The dog's turning was our lullaby.
Each plant and their water asking.
The mountain and its anvil ring. Until
the sky runs out or we aren't sure
we remember it right: was it round
when we held warm beets? Is the kettle
made of steam? This is how it works
for the children of orphans. There was
a story there. But the sky remains.
Speak to that.
            In the new time, everyone will want
a sky of their own. They will need a gun to find it.

Open the round like a window, and the bullet
passes through. Perhaps the next sky
is better. Each new sky has fewer details
than the one before it. In the new sky
of sky, the details are erased until all people
could be the same person: part of a hand
with the thing it holds blown through.
Behind, it is coming: more sky. A time full
of sky. It asks for the gun to make itself.

Sky builds up around the way we have learned
to love in reverse: dear lost you and you and you.

It grows itself like children and feeds them
because it understands from us
how love populates itself.
When I unbind myself from the sky
it goes on standing. Any one of us can open
into next sky at the moment of another's choosing,
and what remains is more. And what remains
is the first round, which returns to iron
and singing, shoe cradle, tree mirror,
bird silver, and engine spark. And more sky
coming. And asking for its making.

4.

TO NAME THIS SPILLING

The engine block, the way
it spreads itself onto the floor.
Power is a built thing—
an engine or a bird the way it is defeathered.
We build by tearing apart.

The day is ablaze.
The president's mouth bleeds fire
over the cities.

Where he assesses,
riots bloom their flowers of hope.

I used to like explosions because they were nothing
like the life I live.
In the morning I see our president

has told his followers to take more men
apart, to take the women. Still. We spill
like spent gauze onto the floors
of our cities and warn our children
of how easily the body is ruined.

The day is on fire from here to the sun.

My chest. My chest.
Where my daughter used to sleep.

I love the earth of this earth.
I love its worms, its golden hungry bees.

ETYMOLOGY OF THE BOMB

Everyone opens the newspaper
/

Radio static   the ashes of sound
speak the disorganization of our bones

Dear Once, Had you heard of the island?

Dear Once,   how the trees emptied their birds
even when the fruit came in

Dear Once, The children hadn't heard of cellar,
hadn't worshipped   salt

     possible to eat the last of a thing
and not think to wash   from your hands

We open the newspaper: the sound // of news
in the turning of the page

We open the paper: the space

Eating is a ritual: bow to grasshopper
         : ask the rare dog to close its eyes

If you move the blast center a little to the south
your sister

TO GLISTEN IMPORTANTLY

My daughter reads me the article
about how people find themselves
five times better looking
when they see themselves in the mirror
than they look in real life.

She reads me this as I look in the mirror. I try
to see my five-times worse-looking self
by remembering the last time I had a hangover
and a migraine. I line the house
with mirrors and invite all the neighbors over.

In the mirrors of the dining room, people five times
better looking than we are
talk and chew and spit gristle at the plates.
I love the way our hands glisten importantly
with grease, how out hair drifts like melancholy
through the sauce. This goes on for decades.

If one of us falls over we can hold a mirror
to check for gorgeous breath.

NOT WORRIED ABOUT THE LOOSENING

The dead walk in the rain, walk under
each drop not worrying
about their loosening
scalps, the hairs thinned from
all the passing through.

And they are loved—mainly by children
because the dead do what children admire most:
pass a pin through the hand,
bloom shrapnel from their guts,

                    wave to a bird and catch fire.

No one interrupts the dead to save them.

Can you see where they press close
to our mouths, enjoying the good wetness
of our breath, the saliva clung with light?

I've noticed how in front of me the dead open
their arms to hold me and more than me.

They hold everything at once simply
by opening: the bicycle and its orange joy,
the truck and its accident, the cage
and the dog of its sadness, the salt,
a whole library asleep in their arms.
I learned from the dead how
to hold the world because they let me watch
and do not require that we look away.

You can walk like that too:

holding everything, open armed, walking
over coals or through the stitches
of your own clothing. If you wish
to hold trees, first choose the one

and walk in. Walk right in.

THE POSSIBLE FORM OF TOMORROW

How did it happen I became good for the midnight call? Me,
not long ago lifting a ruined white pigeon from the stone staircase

on Emerson Street and petting rain and mites from its feathers
until my sister found me there and removed it from my arms

to make room for me to hold myself, weeping until morning struck
to show us we were all still there. I was never the one

my friends would call at night to say how the temple
of their marriage was shaken. But eventually—

and for doing nothing more than stringing enough words together
in the right order and not spilling too often

on the tablecloth of my intention—my phone rings again
at midnight. I hear how the body hurts most

where it has not been touched and that it no longer feels possible
to make it past the shorelined birds of oil.

No one notices when I begin again to dread how the deer
are pressing themselves too close to the edge of my headlights.

The time never seems right
to mention the physicist's theory that we are holograms

bounced off the surface of a membrane in a dimension
we can't confirm exists—I meant to have more source than that.

I meant to live so fiercely my teeth could not live close to my tongue.
Yet the phone rings again, and I answer.

The satellite overhead tethers my breath
to the voice at the other end. Each spoken thing is a harness

to morning, which is far away, but promised, which is far away,
but coming with the light by which we'll assess the remains.

GODS OF THE COUNTERFEIT SKY

We'd meet at the door of his shared house
and head to his rented room with a blanket for a bed.
I was so new to sex I assumed everyone spent

a few years doing it on the floor
or in gas station bathrooms

as a way to pay their dues.

For months he'd emptied his change on the floor
so by the time I got there

it was the cheapest constellation
in the world, making us gods
of a counterfeit sky.

We lay vastly down upon it.
We ruled over Minor Ursa Minor, over
Even Smaller Dipper, Orion the Forager.

My sticky skin gathered coins like a juke box
and then sounds came out.

My back took pennies and dimes.
Quarters rained from my thighs.
Urgent constellations aligned
and I hung over the entire world
answering prayers.

I rolled through that time like a god
gathering the terrible loneliness
of finally calling it quits on creation
so it can start going wrong
on its own.

Even now I find the fallen change
glittering up from gutters and parking lots
in nearly every city.

A POET SHOUTING UP THROUGH THE GRAVES OF POETS
CAN HEAR THE DIRT

Checking out a used piano for a friend,
I had no idea what I was supposed to listen for,
if it was any good or not. As the Russian
played it, he said I should notice how the piano sounded
like night, if the night
were velvet, said it held the important memories
of centuries and helped him find his heart.

The problem is not that we have killed all of the poets
and the ones who spoke the truth.
It is that the sheltered heart remains sheltered.

THE BRICKS WILL BE TAKEN AWAY AND USED AGAIN AS BRICKS

They shut off the water, so we gathered to sinks

our voices white in the tiled spaces

Then the electricity and so we approached the sockets

with static in our hair, appliances outstretched When

they took the windows, we pressed ourselves

to the walls, became doors of each other's passing

Our voices were sewn into quilted sacks, abandoning

the teeth We gathered to the tongue

and our hands We gathered When they take us

from each other, we will join the mirrors

where we will come to know how we meet ourselves

THE EXTRAVAGANCE OF SKY

I arrived on time
to the ghost town.

To have more in common
with the dead, I covered myself with earth

but could feel it already had
too many of us stuck

inside of it. I hadn't thought
of the world like a throat before.

Everyone wanted to watch
the trees full of cellos

play the names of the living.
I took air from the palace of my lungs

and gave it to the next world.
We went on like this sharing extravagances.

They showed me how if you make a bowl
and give it to the sky

the sky can fill it with self, not losing any
and without any left over.

I never want to stop
being amazed by that.

THE GREAT BEAUTIES

The wind blew over the dried lakebed
and raised a curtain of dust.
I wanted to head into it with vast, Pleistocene thoughts,
to go in and come out and be different.

To get there I would need to become the speck of myself
in my own distance, a lakebed stretch of silence.

Walking toward the curtain of dust,
I believed it was possible to become a glorious nothing
but instead all I could think about was the face
of some ruined actor whose name I couldn't remember.

His hair assembled out of light, some dirt.

The faraway wall of dust was a slow procession
of mist bodies. An animal memory of time.

I think in the time of animal departures.

All across the top of the playa
was a fine alkaline lace
raised by the last night's rain.
The lace was laid out like a dress.
Even dirt wants to be beautiful. Even mud
can become a gown for the sun
and ask to be counted
among the great beauties.

The actor I couldn't recall has a head injury
and now does reality TV
where I'm told his damage is hilarious.

I have misunderstood so much of this world:
alkaline mud makes a lace,

dust is the shawl I've been wearing,

even Coney Island white fish—
the despised floating condoms of the boardwalk—
desire a better name in hopes of achieving beyond themselves.

Have you seen the moon's recognition in their paleness?

Then I remembered something else about the actor.
I could see his mouth:
it pressed up to my memory like a sky
pressed up to the memory of its own body.

That mouth had been summoned from the center of dust, recalled
upon the gorgeous lace of mud.

The lace was delicate and would not last
the wind of the evening, but for that moment it was bride
to an autumn sun, and somewhere the used white fish
floated around the ankles of tourists and told them
to behold their distant moons.

ACKNOWLEDGMENTS

Grateful acknowledgment to the editors of the following publications in which these poems first appeared, often in different forms:

Basalt Magazine "So Shiny It Is Hard to Believe," "The Great Beauties," "The Possible Form of Tomorrow," and "In My Original Kansas, When We Were Iron"
Pangea "After Fifteen Years, I Write about My Home"
Solstice Literary Magazine "The Complication of Multiple Lives"
Southern Humanities Review "Lunar Year of the Explosion" and "First Penis"
Writing for Peace "What We Did Instead"
Level Land: Poems For and About the I35 Corridor "In My Original Kansas, When We Were Iron"

Jennifer Oakes' previous works include two award-winning books of poetry and a novel. A frequent collaborator with visual artists, her work has also appeared on sculptures involving license plates, bridges, and columnar basalt. A Minnesota native, Jennifer now lives in Seattle. .